Linking Land-Use Projections and Forest Fragmentation Analysis

ANDREW J. PLANTINGA, RALPH J. ALIG, HENRY EICHMAN, AND DAVID J. LEWIS

A Technical Document Supporting
the USDA Forest Service Interim Update of the 2000 RPA Assessment

U.S. DEPARTMENT OF AGRICULTURE   FOREST SERVICE

Authors

Andrew J. Plantinga is an associate professor, Department of Agricultural and Resource Economics, Oregon State University, Corvallis, OR 97331; **Ralph J. Alig** is a team leader and research forester, U.S. Department of Agriculture, Forest Service, Pacific Northwest Research Station, Forestry Sciences Laboratory, 3200 SW Jefferson Way, Corvallis, OR 97331; **Henry Eichman** is an economist, U.S. Department of the Interior, Bureau of Land Management, Prineville District, 3050 NE Third, Prineville, OR 97754; **David J. Lewis** is an assistant professor, Department of Agricultural and Applied Economics, University of Wisconsin, Madison, WI 53706.

Abstract

Plantinga, Andrew J.; Alig, Ralph J.; Eichman, Henry; Lewis, David J. 2007.
Linking land-use projections and forest fragmentation analysis. Res. Pap. PNW-RP-570. Portland, OR: U.S. Department of Agriculture, Forest Service, Pacific Northwest Station. 41 p.

An econometric model of private land-use decisions is used to project land use to 2030 for each county in the continental United States. On a national scale, forest area is projected to increase overall between 0.1 and 0.2 percent per year between now and 2030. However, forest area is projected to decrease in a majority of regions, including the key forestry regions of the South and the Pacific Northwest Westside. Urban area is projected to increase by 68 million acres, and cropland, pasture, rangeland, and Conservation Reserve Program land is projected to decline in area. Regional econometric models are needed to better represent region-specific economic relationships. County-level models of forest fragmentation indices are estimated for the Western United States. The core forest model is found to perform better than the model of like adjacencies for forest land. A spatially detailed analysis of forest fragmentation in Polk County, Oregon, reveals that forests become more fragmented even though forest area increases. By linking the land-use projection and forest fragmentation models, we project increases in the average county shares of core forest in 8 of the 11 Western States. The average like adjacency measure increases in six of the states. The aggregate and spatially detailed fragmentation methods are compared by projecting the fragmentation indices to 2022 for Polk County, Oregon. Considerable differences in the results were produced with the two methods, especially in the case of the like adjacency metric.

Keywords: Land use, forest-land area, forest fragmentation, spatial analysis.

Contents

Chapter 1: Introduction

The fragmentation of forests into smaller patches affects habitat quality and thus biological diversity, and increases the likelihood of invasion by exotic species. Forest fragmentation is widely considered to be a primary threat to terrestrial biodiversity (Armsworth et al. 2004) and is a pervasive feature of U.S. forests. Riitters et al. (2002) found that approximately 62 percent of forest patches in the lower 48 States are located within 164 yards of the nearest edge. Forest fragmentation can result from land-use intensification, such as housing development, or from natural causes, such as expansion of nonforest plant communities. The overall simplification of biological communities may reduce, and make more costly, the goods and services that humans derive from ecosystems.

Although the ecological effects of forest fragmentation have received substantial attention, an understanding of the economic drivers of fragmentation is less developed. Land-use studies supporting the 2005 Renewable Resources Planning Act (RPA) Assessment update indicated that tens of millions of acres of private forest land in the United States could be converted to urban and developed uses over the next 50 years (e.g., Alig and Plantinga 2004, Alig et al. 2004), resulting in more forested areas being surrounded by nonforest areas, or adjacent to houses, streets, parking lots, and malls. The U.S. population is projected to grow by another 120 million people by 2050, with relatively fast growth rates in the Western United States. These results indicate the importance of understanding economic determinants of forest fragmentation in the context of demands on and supplies of renewable resources from the Nation's forests and rangelands.

Questions to answer concerning forest fragmentation include (1) Where, how much, and how is forest fragmentation happening (e.g., natural vs. human causes)? (2) What factors are causing forest fragmentation? (3) Are fragmentation trends changing (e.g., accelerating)? (4) What are prospective changes in forest fragmentation? (5) What incentives or associated policies could effectively be used to address fragmentation? Our study addresses a number of the questions posed above in the context of forests in the Western United States. We focus on forest fragmentation resulting from land use,[1] directing our attention to the effect of human land uses on forest fragmentation.[2] Land-use changes can result when supplies of land for

Land use changes can result when supplies of land for different uses change in response to economic incentives, changing laws and regulations, and environmental conditions, interacting with shifts in demands for land in response to changes in socioeconomic factors such as population and personal income.

---

[1] Because forest harvesting is often followed by reforestation (Alig and Butler 2004), effects of such age-class fragmentation are often not as severe in the longer term as, for example, conversion of forests to other land uses such as urban development.

[2] We omit from the analysis fragmentation resulting from natural processes such as succession. Moreover, land-cover changes (e.g., timber harvesting) that do not involve changes in land use are not treated as fragmentation.

different uses change in response to economic incentives, changing laws and regulations, and environmental conditions, interacting with shifts in demands for land in response to changes in socioeconomic factors such as population and personal income. Most public forests are unfragmented, whereas urbanization and increasing intensity of land use may lead to more fragmentation of private lands. We, therefore, focus our analysis on the link between land-use changes on private lands and forest fragmentation.

Our study of forest fragmentation supports the Sustainable Wood Production Initiative (SWPI) (Deal and White 2005) and the 2005 update of the 2000 RPA assessment (USDA Forest Service 2001), which was prepared in response to the mandate in the Forest and Rangeland Renewable Resources Planning Act of 1974, P.L. 93-378, 88 Stat. 475, as amended (RPA). Both the SWPI and RPA Assessments seek to better understand the major economic, ecological, and social issues affecting sustainable forestry. The 1974 RPA legislation established a periodic reporting requirement and broadened the resource coverage from timber alone to all renewable resources (e.g., fish and wildlife) from U.S. forests and associated issues such as fragmentation of forested landscapes. Fragmentation concerns are now also being reflected in the design of conservation policies in the most recent U.S. Farm Bill. For example, reducing forest fragmentation is a primary goal in the Wildlife Habitat Incentives Program as administered by several states. Likewise, many wildlife conservation plans adopted or proposed by nongovernmental agencies such as Partners-In-Flight have explicit goals related to the reduction of forest fragmentation.

Conservation and management of U.S. forests is based in part on international protocols (e.g., Montreal Process), which are intended to provide a common understanding of what is meant by sustainable forest management and to provide a common framework for describing, assessing, and evaluating a country's progress toward sustainability at the national level. For example, one criterion is maintenance and enhancement of long-term multiple socioeconomic benefits to meet the needs of societies. Clearly, the provision of these benefits is affected by forest fragmentation. However, the associated indicators, such as one for forest fragmentation (Riitters et al. 2002), offer little information about population and income and other drivers of change in resource conditions. In our study, we augment efforts such as the Montreal Process by reporting on important drivers of change in resource conditions and how issues such as urbanization crosscut or affect many measures of U.S. renewable resource condition, particularly forest fragmentation.

The design of our study is illustrated in figure 1 (the ovals represent components of the study; the boxes are inputs and outputs). The first component is a

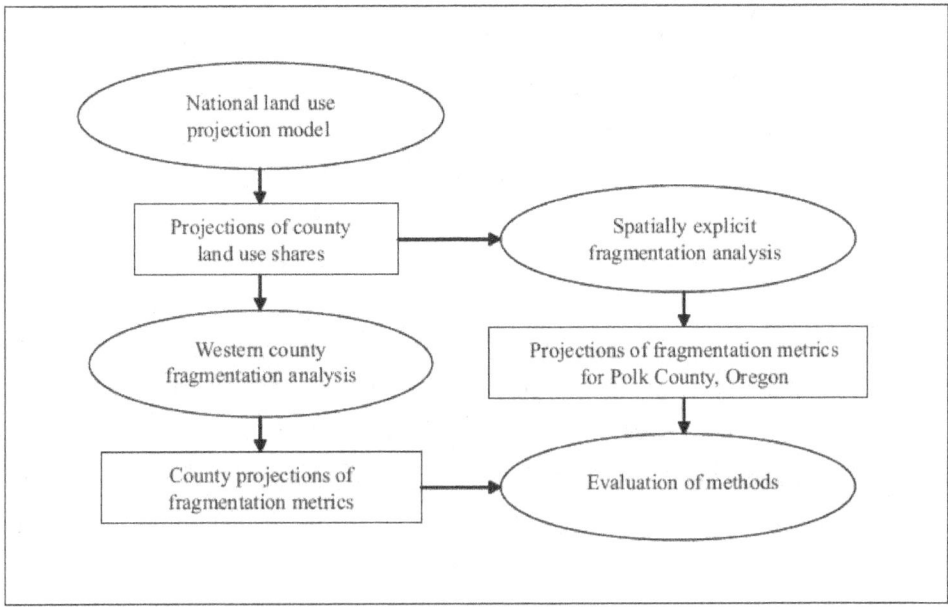

Figure 1—An illustration of the study design.

national-level land-use projection model based on an econometric analysis of land use changes among crop, pasture, forest, urban, Conservation Reserve Program, and range categories. The econometric model is estimated with data on nonfederal land and explains land-use changes in terms of economic returns and site characteristics such as land quality. The projection model is used to generate land-use projections, by county, to 2030. We use forest fragmentation metrics (the share of the landscape in core forest and the percentage of like adjacencies) to characterize the amount of forest fragmentation in the Western United States. A statistical analysis is undertaken to explain the observed variation across counties in these metrics. These results support a linking of the land-use projections and the aggregate fragmentation analysis, allowing us to estimate how the fragmentation metrics may change as the shares of land in different uses differ. Chapter 4 contains a spatially explicit analysis of forest fragmentation in Polk County, Oregon. Projections of fragmentation metrics are generated and compared to those produced by the aggregate data approach used in chapter 3. This comparison sheds light on tradeoffs between precision and costs of data collection, assembly, and processing at different scales of inquiry. We conclude by summarizing key findings and offering suggestions for further research.

Chapter 2: National Econometric Model

Lubowski et al. (2006) conducted a national-scale analysis of the cost of sequestering carbon in forests. As part of this project, Lubowski (2002) developed a national-scale econometric model of land use. Lubowski estimated the probabilities for transitions between six major land-use categories. The transition probabilities are functions of net financial returns to the alternative uses, soil quality, and estimated parameters. The first step in the present research is to incorporate the econometric results into a land-use projection model. The projection model is an algorithm that projects changes in land use, beginning with 1997 base year conditions. The model treats crop and timber prices as endogenous, thereby accounting for feedback effects of land-use change on the prices of key commodities. The following sections describe Lubowski's econometric model and the algorithm used for the land-use projections and present and discuss national and regional land-use projections to 2030.

Methods

Econometric Land-Use Model

The National Resources Inventory (NRI) is the primary data set used by Lubowski (2002) to estimate a national econometric land-use model. The NRI is a panel survey of land use and land characteristics on nonfederal lands conducted at 5-year intervals from 1982 to 1997 over the entire United States, excluding Alaska. Data include approximately 844,000 plot-level observations, each representing a land area given by a sampling weight. The NRI provides information on three land-use transitions over the periods 1982-87, 1987-92, and 1992-97. The Lubowski analysis focuses on the lower 48 States and six major land uses: crops, pasture, forest, urban, range, and Conservation Reserve Program (CRP).[3] The land base in the study comprises 1.4 billion acres, representing about 74 percent of the total land area and about 91 percent of nonfederal land in the contiguous United States.

The dependent variable in the econometric model is the choice of land use in year $t+5$ ($t = 1982, 1987, 1992$) at each NRI plot, and the independent variables are the land use in year t, the land quality rating of the plot, and proxies for the expected net returns from the land-use alternatives as of year t. By assembling data

---

[3] Lands in "rural roads and transportation" uses are likely to change through a different decisionmaking process than profit maximization by private landowners, and are omitted. Streams and water bodies, marshlands, and barren lands are also excluded, as these uses are unlikely to differ over time. Finally, lands classified under unspecified "miscellaneous" uses are omitted.

from a variety of private and public sources, Lubowski (2002) constructed county-level estimates of annual net returns (per acre) for crops, pasture, forest, range, and urban uses for all 3,014 counties in the 48 contiguous states.[4] The net returns to cropland and timber are weighted averages of net returns to specific crops and forest types, where the weights reflect current cropping patterns and forest type distributions (see the appendix for more details). The land quality measure is the land capability class (LCC) rating of the NRI plot. The LCC rating is a composite index representing 12 factors (e.g., soil type, slope) that determine the suitability of the land for agriculture. It also serves as a proxy measure for forest productivity. The LCC rating ranges from I to VIII, where I indicates the greatest potential for intensive agricultural uses. For the econometric analysis, the eight LCC categories are combined to produce four land quality classes. [5]

Landowners are assumed to have static expectations of future net financial returns and to allocate their land to the use generating the highest return net of conversion costs. Net financial returns are assumed to have deterministic and random components. The deterministic component includes the county net return, land quality class dummy variables (**LQ**), and the interaction between the two variables. This specification allows for plot-level deviations from the average county return. Certain distributional assumptions (see Train 2003) are imposed on the random components of net returns to yield a nested logit model for estimation. Three nests include land uses with similar land quality requirements: crops, pasture, and CRP; forest and range; and urban.[6] Details on the econometric estimation and results are available in Lubowski (2002) and Lubowski et al. (2006). The analysis yields probabilities for transitions between each of the six land uses. These probabilities are functions of independent variables and estimated parameters,

$$P_{ijkt} = P(\hat{\beta}_{jk}, \mathbf{NR}_{it}, \mathbf{LQ}_i) \tag{1}$$

where P_{ijkt} denotes the probability that plot i transitions from use j to k during the interval beginning in year t, $\hat{\beta}_{jk}$ is a vector of estimated parameters for the j to k transition, $\mathbf{NR}_{it}$ is a vector of net returns to the six uses in year t and for the county

---

[4] Net returns estimates are, thus, constructed for all of the land-use categories, except for CRP, which is modeled by using a different procedure discussed in Lubowski (2002).

[5] Land quality class 1 includes LCC I and II land, land quality class 2 includes LCC III and IV land, land quality class 3 includes LCC V and VI land, and land quality class 4 includes LCC VII and VIII land.

[6] Crops, pasture, and CRP lands tend to have relatively high quality (in terms of the LCC rating), whereas forest and range lands have relatively low quality. There is little correspondence between urban uses and land quality and so urban is placed in a separate nest.

where plot i is located, and $\mathbf{LQ}_i$ is a vector of land quality class dummy variables for plot i.[7]

Land-Use Projection Model

The key inputs to the land-use projection model are the transition probabilities in (1) and plot-level data on land use, net returns, and soil quality from the NRI. The projection model operates at the NRI plot level and begins in the base year 1997. To simplify notation, we denote the years 1997, 2002, and 2007, etc., as $t = 0, 1,$ 2, etc. Based on the sampling design, each NRI plot is associated with a certain number of acres. We define A_{ijt} as the number of acres associated with plot i in use j in time t. In the initial period, each plot is in one of the six uses as indicated in the 1997 NRI data. Thus, A_{ij0} equals the acres represented by plot i if the plot is in use j in time 0, and equals 0 otherwise. Given a sequence of transition probabilities, we can compute how this land will be distributed across the six use categories at each time in the future. We can then express the area of land represented by plot i that transitions (transition acres) from use j to k during the interval beginning in t as $TA_{ijkt} = P_{ijkt} \cdot A_{ijt}$. As well, the acres of land represented by plot i in use j at time $t+1$ are given by,

$$A_{ijt+1} = \sum_k TA_{ikjt} = \sum_k P_{ikjt} \cdot A_{ikt} \qquad (2)$$

This expression reflects the first-order Markov structure of our model.

The transition probabilities in the base year are computed with the 1997 values of the net returns (and the time-independent coefficients, $\hat{\beta}_{jk}$, and variables, LLC_i). With the initial acres A_{ij0}, we can estimate the acres in each use in time 1 by using the relationship in (2). The induced change in land use implies a change in the supply of land-based commodities and services and, hence, changes in related prices and the net returns from each use. We model these endogenous price effects for forest and cropland, and assume the net returns to pasture, range, urban, and the CRP remain constant throughout the simulation. Pasture and CRP account for a small share of the total land base. Rangeland is a major component of the land base (about 30 percent initially), but we were unable to find any information on markets (specifically, demand elasticities) for forage, the principal output of range-land. Finally, the probabilities for transitions into urban uses were found to be insensitive to changes in urban rents, indicating that these transition probabilities would tend to remain the same even with endogenous price effects.

> The key inputs to the land-use projection model are the transition probabilities in (1) and plot-level data on land use, net returns, and soil quality from the NRI.

---

[7] Conversion costs are not measured explicitly, but rather are reflected in constant terms specific to each land-use transition.

Consistent with the model of landowner behavior underlying the econometric analysis, cropland and forest commodities are supplied inelastically. Thus, we can use crop and timber yields, measured in output per acre, to translate land-use changes into output changes. After aggregating output changes to the appropriate level, we compute corresponding price changes by using own-price demand elasticities estimated in previous econometric studies.[8] Changes in cropland area result in immediate changes in crop output because crops are assumed to be harvested in the same year that they are planted. In the case of forests, timber harvests will be delayed for a period of years while the forest stand grows to maturity. For afforested lands, we assume that harvests are delayed for the period of one optimal rotation, after which time the forest is "fully regulated" and provides a constant annual flow of timber.[9] Likewise, all land originally in forest (i.e., in $t = 0$) is assumed to have a fully regulated structure. When these lands are converted to nonforest uses, we assume that only a portion of the timber (20 percent) is merchantable.

The assumption of a fully regulated forest will clearly overstate the timber supply from private forests. It is well documented that nonindustrial private landowners, who own almost 80 percent of the private forest in the United States, frequently manage their lands for nontimber outputs such as recreation (Butler and Leatherberry 2004). To account for these alternative management objectives, we assume that a fixed percentage of forest land in each timber production region (see footnote 4) is never harvested, while the remaining forest is harvested in the manner described above. The no-harvest percentages are determined by calibrating the model to regional timber harvest data for 1997.[10] The no-harvest percentages range from 6 percent in the South Central region to 62 percent in the Pacific Southwest region.

Once we have computed the price changes resulting from the land-use changes between periods 0 and 1, we can form new measures of net returns in period 1. Specifically, we apply the national or regional percentage price change to the

---

[8] For crop commodities, we use a national-level demand elasticity for raw food inputs by food processors (Goodwin and Brester 1995). We apply this elasticity (-0.661) separately to each of the 25 crop commodities in our model. For timber, we use demand elasticities for seven timber production regions—Pacific Northwest (-0.300), Pacific Southwest (-0.497), Rocky Mountains (-0.054), North Central (-0.141), Northeast (-0.029), South Central (-0.193), Southeast (-0.285)—from the Timber Assessment Market Model (Adams and Haynes 1996). These elasticities apply to a composite timber type representative of the species found within the region. In general, we would expect the mixes of crop and timber types to change in response to price changes. However, we assume for simplicity that the crop and timber type shares remain constant over time.

[9] Specifically, if t^* is the optimal rotation length, then there is an equal area of forest in each age category in the interval $[0, t^*]$. Each year, timber of age t^*, or $1/t^*$ of the forest area, is harvested.

[10] These data were provided to the authors by Dr. Darius Adams in the Department of Forest Resources at Oregon State University.

county-level prices used to compute net returns. With the period 1 net returns, we recalculate the transition probabilities and repeat the procedure. This stage of the simulation ends when the crop and forest net returns have converged (i.e., period-to-period changes in prices are near zero). The converged net returns are equilibrium values that reflect all anticipated supply adjustments in agricultural and forest commodity markets. This process is atemporal; it represents an instantaneous adjustment to a new market equilibrium. For this reason, we hold urban land constant during this stage of the simulation. Urban land will increase over time with factors such as population growth—as it does in the second stage of the algorithm discussed below—but should not affect the immediate adjustment in net returns to cropland and forests.

In the second stage of the algorithm, we compute the time path of land-use changes. Specifically, we recalculate the transition probabilities for the initial period by using the converged net returns for cropland and forests and the observed net returns for the other uses. Beginning with the initial acres in each use (A_{ij0}), we use (2) to compute the sequence of land-use transitions (TA_{ijkt}) through time. Unlike in the first stage of the algorithm, the net returns remain at their equilibrium values throughout this stage.

Projection Results

Lubowski (2002) developed two sets of econometric results. One set uses data on transitions from all three periods and the other uses data only on transitions from the final period (1992–97). We generated projections with both sets of estimates, but present here only the results based on the 1992-1997 parameters as similar results are obtained. Table 1 shows the national-level changes.[11] Forest area is projected to increase between 0.1 and 0.2 percent per year from 1997 to 2030. The largest increases occur between now and 2010 and, then, gradually decline. Urban land shows the largest increase of any use category. The overall net increase in national forest area represents a 4.7 percent increase between 1997 and 2030, in contrast to a 1.5 percent decrease projected by Alig et al. (2003) using a mixture of databases. The NRI data on land use transactions among major land uses analyzed in the current study allow projections of net changes as well as gross land-use changes, e.g., the total amount of forest area projected to be deforested.

Urban area increases by approximately 2 million acres per year throughout the projection period, for a total gain of 68 million acres by 2030. This represents an average annual increase of 2.7 percent. The increases in forest and urban area

---

[11] Some of the following results were presented in an earlier publication by Alig and Plantinga (2004).

Table 1—Land-use projections for the contiguous United States, 1997 to 2030

Year	Cropland	Pasture	Forest	Urban	CRP	Rangeland	Total
			Land uses				
Area projections			*1,000 acres*				
1997	376,383	119,513	404,680	75,924	32,696	404,824	1,414,019
2002	369,364	129,912	408,668	86,056	27,262	392,758	1,414,019
2010	362,828	125,431	414,652	103,007	22,661	385,440	1,414,019
2020	354,061	119,016	419,905	123,777	19,098	378,162	1,414,019
2030	344,911	113,209	423,464	143,969	16,789	371,677	1,414,019
Change, 1997-2030	-31,472	-6,303	18,784	68,045	-15,907	-33,147	
Annual change			*1,000 acres per year*				
1997-2002	-1,404	2,080	798	2,026	-1,087	-2,413	
2002-2010	-817	-560	748	2,119	-575	-915	
2010-2020	-877	-642	525	2,077	-356	-728	
2020-2030	-915	-581	356	2,019	-231	-648	
Annual percent change			*Percent per year*				
1997-2002	-0.4	1.7	0.2	2.7	-3.3	-0.6	
2002-2010	-0.2	-0.4	0.2	2.5	-2.1	-0.2	
2010-2020	-0.2	-0.5	0.1	2.0	-1.6	-0.2	
2020-2030	-0.3	-0.5	0.1	1.6	-1.2	-0.2	

CRP = Conservation Reserve Program.

come at the expense of cropland, pasture, CRP, and rangeland, which are projected to decline, respectively, by 31.4, 6.3, 15.9, and 33.1 million acres by 2030. With the exception of pasture area, which increases initially, the largest declines in these categories occur between now and 2010.

Table 2 disaggregates the national projections by RPA regions.[12] Forest area is projected to decrease in a majority of regions, including the key forestry regions of the South and the Pacific Northwest Westside. The table reveals increases in forest area in five regions (Pacific Northwest East, Mountain, Northern Plains, Corn Belt, and South Plains) and declines in forest area in six regions (Pacific Southwest, Pacific Northwest West, Lake States, Northeast, Southeast, and South Central). The largest increases are projected in the Mountain, North Plains, Cornbelt, and South

Forest area is projected to decrease in a majority of regions, including the key forestry regions of the South and the Pacific Northwest Westside.

[12] The regions include the following states or the indicated portions thereof: PSW (CA), PNWW (western OR and WA), PNWE (eastern OR and WA), Mountain (AZ, CO, ID, MT, NM, NV, UT, WY), Northern Plains (KS, NB, ND, SD), South Plains (western OK and TX), Lake States (MI, MN, WI), Corn Belt (IA, IL, IN, MO, OH), South Central (AL, AR, KY, LA, MS, eastern OK, TN, eastern TX), Northeast (CT, DE, MA, MD, ME, NH, NJ, NY, PA, RI, VT, WV), and Southeast (FL, GA, NC, SC, VA).

Table 2—Regional land-use projections for the contiguous United States, 1997 to 2030

Region	Land uses					
	Cropland	Pasture	Forest	Urban	CRP	Rangeland
Change, 1997-2030			*1,000 acres*			
Pacific Southwest	-1,742	1,402	-594	5,748	-114	-4,701
Pacific Northwest West	-545	-932	-1,883	3,120	8	232
Pacific Northwest East	-3,113	2,793	2,048	2,634	-1,289	-3,072
Mountain	-3,098	7,408	10,313	8,942	-2,912	-20,653
Northern Plains	-12,123	8,179	5,703	6,298	-3,407	-4,651
Lake States	-3,978	-282	-1,240	5,290	-1,423	1,633
Corn Belt	-8,441	-4,494	5,416	7,365	-3,171	3,325
Northeast	-3,988	-1,860	-2,980	7,073	19	1,735
Southeast	-224	-3,158	-3,606	6,996	-780	772
South Plains	739	440	8,005	5,083	-2,009	-2,259
South Central	5,041	-15,800	-2,399	9,496	-829	4,492
All regions	-31,472	-6,303	18,784	68,045	-15,907	-33,147
Percentage change, 1997-2030	*Percent*					
Pacific Southwest	-18.1	133.7	-4.3	119.8	-65.7	-25.7
Pacific Northwest West	-39.1	-58.8	-12.0	172.6	724.4	389.7
Pacific Northwest East	-34.5	178.0	21.1	416.5	-86.0	-20.4
Mountain	-8.4	88.3	40.1	185.9	-46.0	-11.1
Northern Plains	-13.8	111.1	170.5	294.1	-39.7	-6.5
Lake States	-9.8	-3.3	-2.6	82.6	-56.3	N/A
Corn Belt	-9.6	-21.6	18.5	73.4	-66.4	3,800.5
Northeast	-24.8	-24.7	-3.8	51.6	9.8	N/A
Southeast	-1.2	-23.7	-4.8	45.8	-66.1	23.9
South Plains	2.1	2.8	199.8	83.2	-40.0	-11.3
South Central	15.4	-47.0	-2.3	93.0	-34.2	350.2
All regions	-8.4	-5.3	4.6	89.6	-48.7	-8.2

Plains regions, and are accompanied by large declines in rangeland in the Mountain and South Plains regions and cropland in the North Plains and Cornbelt regions. The largest declines in forest area are projected in the Northeast, Southeast, and South Central regions. In all regions, the area of urban land increases significantly. Cropland area declines in all but the South Plains and South Central regions. Pasture and rangeland gain or lose area depending on the region.

We project relatively large increases in forest area in regions—Mountain, North Plains, Cornbelt, and South Plains —not normally considered to have active margins between forest and nonforest uses. We consider two possible explanations. First, the

Table 3—Observed land-use transitions to and from forest, 1992 to 1997

Region	Land-use transitions		
	Pasture to forest	**Range to forest**	**Forest to nonforest**
	1,000 acres		
Pacific Southwest	19	398	741
Pacific Northwest West	17	0	148
Pacific Northwest East	11	93	32
Mountain	13	820	462
Northern Plains	20	42	56
Lake States	583	0	404
Corn Belt	1,128	7	608
Northeast	972	0	1,376
Southeast	732	105	2,555
South Plains	358	99	74
South Central	2,254	23	1,876

econometric results that underlie the projections were part of a national analysis. In particular, a single set of parameters was estimated to characterize the observed land-use patterns. The model may be able to accurately represent land-use trends at a national scale because it reflects the central tendency of the data. However, it may be less accurate at a regional level because the model is not specified to capture regional differences in the underlying relationships. This represents a potential limitation of the fragmentation analyses presented in chapters 3 and 4, which draw on regional land-use projections.

To a significant degree, the projections are a reflection of the land-use transitions between 1992 and 1997.[13] Thus, a second possibility is that the regional projections simply mimic the land-use changes that actually occurred during this period. Table 3 presents some evidence in support of this explanation. For each region, it shows the acres of land that moved from pasture to forest, from range to forest, and from forest to nonforest uses (cropland, pasture, urban, etc.). In the Mountain region, a relatively large amount of rangeland (820,000 acres) converted to forest between 1992 and 1997, while a smaller area of land left forest (462,000 acres). A similar pattern is seen in the Cornbelt and South Plains regions, except in these cases there were relatively large amounts of pasture transitioning to forest. In some regions where we project declines in forest, such as the Northeast and Southeast, the flow of land out of forest between 1992 and 1997 exceed the flow of land into forest.

---

[13] Land-use classification is complicated in some regions when relatively small changes in vegetation composition can shift land between uses classes; especially between forestry and pasture or rangeland. Regions where this occurs include the Mountains and Plains regions.

Chapter 3: Western Fragmentation Model

In this chapter, we present aggregate models of forest fragmentation for 11 Western States. Using county-level data, we estimate models of two fragmentation indices, the share of the county in core forest, and the percentage of neighboring parcels that are also forested (like adjacencies). The explanatory variables describe county land-use shares, forest ownership, land quality, topography, the likelihood of changes in forest area, and the income distribution of a county's residents. The purpose of this analysis is to identify the determinants of forest fragmentation by using aggregate data and to develop a model that can be used to project fragmentation indices. The fragmentation indices used as dependent variables summarize the spatial configuration of land use within the county. In chapter 4, we present an analysis of forest fragmentation for a single county that accounts for land-use decisions on individual parcels. This approach offers more precision than the methods described here, but this precision comes at a higher cost in terms of managing large data sets, using specialized software, and requiring greater computing time. If readily available aggregate data can be used to model forest fragmentation, then reliable projections of forest fragmentation can be made at low cost and over large geographical areas.

Butler et al. (2004) and Alig et al. (2005) estimated aggregate models of forest fragmentation in western Washington and western Oregon. The dependent variables used to describe forest fragmentation in these studies included spatial metrics (percentage edge, share of like adjacencies) and aggregate land-use variables (share of nonforest). Both studies use data defined at the census tract scale and consider models with combined and individual spatial metrics. In both studies, population density, share of land in agricultural use, and the distance to highways had statistically significant coefficients. The Butler et al. study also found the share of federal land and slope to be statistically significant. They concluded that their composite index of forest fragmentation is a viable alternative to the multiple metric method used to describe components of forest fragmentation, and that the empirical model conforms to land-use theory. The Alig et al. study found distance to urban centers and the spatial configuration of land quality to be statistically significant across all their models. They found that including the spatial configuration of land quality increased the fit by more when the dependent variable represented a spatial pattern rather than an aggregate land-use share.

Data and Methods

Our study area consists of 11 Western States (Washington, Oregon, California, Idaho, Nevada, Montana, Wyoming, Utah, Arizona, Colorado, and New Mexico).

Counties containing no forest land were eliminated, giving us a total of 372 observations for analysis.

The dependent variables in our study are the share of the county in core forest and the percentage of like adjacencies (neighbors that are like the subject) for forest. These indices are derived from the U.S. Geological Survey National Land Cover Data for the early 1990s.[1] Data representing fragmentation from natural processes are excluded, and temporary land-cover changes (e.g., from timber harvesting) are not treated as fragmentation. The data are delineated in a 100-foot grid. A core forest parcel is defined as a forest parcel at least 100 feet from a nonforest edge. The core forest variable equals the number of core forest parcels in a county divided by the total number of parcels in the county (times 100 to convert the variable to a percentage). It indicates both the amount of forest land in a county and the extent to which these parcels form relatively large blocks of forest. For example, a county would have a low value of this index if it had a large area of forest that is severely fragmented or if it had a small area that formed forest blocks. The core forest share ranges from 0 to 93.5 percent, with a mean of 32.4 percent. Table 4 provides summary statistics for the variables used in this study.

The percentage of like adjacencies for forest is defined as,

$$\frac{100}{N} \sum_{i=1}^{N} \left(\frac{1}{8} \sum_{j=1}^{8} ADJ_{ij} \right), \tag{3}$$

where $I = 1, \ldots, N$ indexes the forested parcels in a county and ADJ_{ij} is an indicator variable that takes the value 1 if the jth parcel adjacent to parcel i is forested and the value 0 if it is not. Adjacency is defined by using an eight-neighbor rule[2] and, thus, the term in parentheses equals the share of parcels adjacent to parcel i that are also forested. These proportions are then averaged over all forested parcels in the county. The percentage of like adjacencies measures the contiguity of forest parcels. It equals 0 if forest parcels are maximally dispersed and tends toward 100 as a county becomes entirely forested. The percentage of like adjacencies ranges from

---

[1] We thank Jennifer Swenson for computing these indices. Because the indices represent forest fragmentation within counties, the metrics may be artificially truncated at the county boundaries. For example, if contiguous forest blocks span county boundaries, the indices will overstate the degree of fragmentation. We do not make adjustments for this problem, but note that the influence of borders is diminished with large counties and small parcel sizes (100-foot grid, in our case).

[2] In a 3 by 3 grid, the center parcel is adjacent to eight neighbors.

Table 4—Ranges and expected signs of variables used in the aggregate forest fragmentation models

Variable	Minimum	Mean	Maximum	Expected sign	
				Core	Like adjacencies
Share of core forest parcels	0	32.4	93.5	N/A	N/A
Share of like adjacent parcels	0	98.2	100.0	N/A	N/A
Share of crops	0	9.2	74.4	-	-
Share of pasture	0	2.5	15.3	-	-
Share of forest	0	14.2	87.3	+	+
Share of urban	0	2.9	58.2	-	-
Share of Conservation Reserve Program	0	1.0	14.7	-	-
Share of range	0	26.6	90.5	-	-
Share of federal forest land	0	22.4	79.0	+	+
Share of nonfederal public forest land	0	2.3	42.6	+	+
Share of nonfederal land in LCC I	0	.7	19.5	+	+
Share of nonfederal land in LCC II	0	4.3	40.5	+	+
Share of nonfederal land in LCC III	0	12.4	63.7	+	+
Share of nonfederal land in LCC IV	0	15.1	70.7	+	+
Share of nonfederal land in LCC V	0	1.2	16.8	+	+
Share of nonfederal land in LCC VI	0	28.2	80.8	+	+
Share of nonfederal land in LCC VII	0	33.8	94.4	+	+
Share of nonfederal land in LCC VIII	0	4.3	42.0	+	+
Range of elevation (in feet)	155.0	1,714.0	4,393.0	-	-
Agriculture-to-forest transition probability	0	0	.3	+	+
Only public forest	0	.1	1.0	+	+
Forest-to-agriculture transition probability	0	0	0	-	-
Forest-to-urban transition probability	0	0	.1	-	-
Share of wealthy households	0	2.3	17.0	-	-

0 to 99.998 percent. The mean is 98.2 percent, indicating that most forest parcels in the study region are surrounded by other forested parcels. The correlation coefficient for the core forest and like adjacencies measures is 42 percent, indicating that the two measures move together but represent different features of fragmentation.

Variation in the county forest fragmentation indices is explained by using a set of independent variables. These variables can be grouped to represent four general factors hypothesized to influence the spatial arrangement of forest land. The first group measures the aggregate allocations of land to forest and alternative uses. The second group accounts for effects of public ownership of forests. The third group measures the influence of land quality, which influences the feasibility of forest and other uses. Finally, the last group summarizes the effect of economic factors such as net returns to alternative land uses. The selection of variables reflects an effort to obtain a predictive model while also yielding insights into the important determinants of forest fragmentation. It is important to emphasize that we model

The selection of variables reflects an effort to obtain a predictive model while also yielding insights into the important determinants of forest fragmentation.

the cross-sectional variation in forest fragmentation. As such, we are interpreting forest fragmentation as a static outcome (i.e., as a state of the landscape). If repeated observations of the fragmentation metrics were available, one could model the dynamic process that leads to fragmentation.

To account for the effect of human land uses on forest fragmentation, the county shares of nonfederal land in forest, crops, pasture, urban, CRP, and range were included as explanatory variables. Data on areas of land in these six major land-use categories were extracted from the 1997 NRI survey results, and land-use shares were calculated as a percentage of total county acreage.[3] We expect that, overall, the forest share will have a positive effect on the fragmentation metrics because both indices tend toward 100 as a county becomes entirely forested. However, depending on how forest land is arranged spatially, it is possible for a county with a greater share of land in forest to have more fragmented forests than another county with less forest land. We expect land in other uses to have a negative effect on the fragmentation indices overall, although, as above, the land-use share variables do not measure the spatial configuration of land uses. Including the county land-use shares in the model enables us to project fragmentation by using the land-use projections from chapter 2.

The NRI data used to measure the land-use shares account only for nonfederal land. We included the shares of federal and nonfederal public forest land (e.g., state and municipal forest land) as additional explanatory variables. Public forest areas were taken from the U.S. Forest Service Forest Inventory Analysis (FIA) Integrated Database (RPA 2002 Tabler/Mapmaker Version 1.0) and calculated as a percentage of total county acreage. The observations are from different FIA survey years ranging from the late 1980s to the mid 1990s. We expect public forests, whether in federal or nonfederal ownerships, to be unfragmented relative to private forests because development and other nonforest uses are typically prohibited on these lands. These variables would also control for nonhuman causes of forest fragmentation (e.g., transition zones between forest and nonforest plant communities) to the extent that these effects are systematic across public forests. Overall, we expect the shares of public forest land to be positively related to the fragmentation metrics.

Land capability class shares were included to capture variation within the county in land quality. The areas of land in each of the eight LCC classes were

---

[3] The land-use shares, and some of the other variables discussed below, are measured a few years after the fragmentation indices. Aggregate land-use measures change very slowly and, thus, we do not expect this to be a problem.

extracted from the 1997 NRI database and then normalized on the area of nonfederal land in each county. Alig et al. (2005) found that indices summarizing the spatial configuration of land quality are an important determinant of forest fragmentation. It was too costly to construct such measures for this study. However, if our non-spatial LCC variables, which are readily computed from NRI data, are significant predictors of forest fragmentation, models of forest fragmentation can be developed at lower cost. Overall, we expect a negative relationship between high-quality land and the fragmentation metrics because high-quality land tends to be allocated to intensive agricultural uses such as crops and pasture. We include dummy variables for LCC classes II through VIII (class I is the omitted category). Because class I is the highest quality land, we expect positive signs on the remaining categories. That is, increasing the share of land in lower quality classes raises the fragmentation metrics relative to class I lands.

To capture the variability of land quality within each county, a variable measuring the range in elevation is included. We conjecture that counties with a large range in elevation should have greater variability in land quality and, as a result, more fragmented forests. The elevation data were extracted from a global scale Digital Elevation Model in ArcGIS[4] and calculated as the difference (in feet) between the maximum and minimum elevations within each county.

Average land-use transition probabilities were calculated for the counties in the study area from the econometric results in chapter 2. The probabilities are for the period 1992 to 1997 and for transitions on nonfederal land from agriculture to forest, forest to agriculture, and forest to urban. These probabilities incorporate the effects of land rents on land-use transitions involving forest land. Land rents, in turn, reflect the drivers of land-use change such as commodity price changes, population growth, and public infrastructure investment.[5] We expect counties with high probabilities for transitions from agriculture to forest to have a higher proportion of core forest and forest parcels with like adjacencies. In this case, conversion of agricultural land to forest may join existing forest parcels, thereby increasing the value of the fragmentation indices. For the opposite reason, counties with high probabilities for transitions from forest to agriculture and urban uses should have more fragmented forests.

---

[4] We thank Scott Walker for providing these data.

[5] Another alternative approach, which we leave for future investigation, would be to enter county land rents directly into the regression equation. This might reduce collinearity with some of the other variables in the model.

The transition probabilities reflect the influence of market forces on land-use change. Because public forests are typically managed for reasons other than maximizing financial returns (e.g., provision of wildlife habitat and recreation), the forest-to-agriculture and forest-to-urban transition probabilities are not applicable to these lands. In a small number of counties, all forests are publicly owned. We construct a dummy variable for these counties, denoted D_{Public}, and enter it in the model as follows,

$$\beta_1 D_{Public} + (1-D_{Public})(\beta_2 P_{FA} + \beta_3 P_{FU}) , \qquad (4)$$

where P_{FA} and P_{FU} are the forest to agriculture and forest to urban transition probabilities and $\beta_1, \beta_2, \beta_3$ are the corresponding coefficients. The influence of having only public forests is measured by β_1, which we expect to be positively signed. The effects of the transition probabilities are measured only for counties with some private forest land because $(1-D_{Public})(\beta_2 P_{FA} + \beta_3 P_{FU})=0$ for counties with only public forests.

Finally, a variable measuring the share of wealthy households was included to test the relationship between income and the resulting lifestyle choices that may influence forest fragmentation. Higher incomes could increase the demand for large-lot housing amenities such as privacy and forested settings. Therefore, counties with a large share of higher income households would be associated with fragmented forests. The share of wealthy households is calculated as the percentage of households in a county with income three or more times the national median household income ($30,056 in 1989). The income data are from the U.S. Bureau of the Census.

We use standard multiple linear regression models to quantify the relationships between the explanatory variables and the two forest fragmentation measures. The dependent variables in our models are shares and, therefore, lie in the unit interval. Predictions from a model estimated with ordinary least squares, however, may fall outside the unit interval. We did not encounter this problem in projecting the fragmentation indices and, therefore, did not pursue alternative estimation approaches. White's (1980) estimate of the covariance matrix was used. This provides consistent estimates of standard errors in the presence of unknown heteroskedasticity.

Results

The estimation results for the core forest model are presented in table 5. The adjusted R-squared statistic indicates that the explanatory variables explain

Table 5—Estimation results for the core forest model

Variable	Coefficient	Standard error	t-value	P-value
Intercept	-36.11**	16.38	-2.21	0.028
Share of crops	0.03	0.04	0.63	0.528
Share of pasture	0.24	0.16	1.47	0.142
Share of forest	0.89**	0.04	25.53	<0.001
Share of urban	-0.07	0.09	-0.75	0.454
Share of Conservation Reserve Program	-0.050.17	-0.32		0.752
Share of range	0.01	0.03	0.43	0.667
Share of federal forest land	0.84**	0.03	27.08	<0.001
Share of nonfederal public forest land	0.19**	0.09	2.13	0.034
Share of nonfederal land in LCC II	0.34*	0.19	1.82	0.069
Share of nonfederal land in LCC III	0.30*	0.16	1.82	0.069
Share of nonfederal land in LCC IV	0.35**	0.17	2.11	0.036
Share of nonfederal land in LCC V	0.21	0.20	1.01	0.311
Share of nonfederal land in LCC VI	0.36**	0.16	2.23	0.027
Share of nonfederal land in LCC VII	0.36**	0.16	2.21	0.028
Share of nonfederal land in LCC VIII	0.24	0.17	1.47	0.143
Per-county range of elevation	.001	.001	1.00	0.32
Agriculture-to-forest transition probability	27.89**	9.43	2.96	0.003
Only public forest	-2.05	2.81	-0.73	0.466
Forest-to-agriculture transition probability	76.25	295.12	0.26	0.796
Forest-to-urban transition probability	-33.92	75.72	-0.45	0.654
Share of wealthy households	.09	.35	.26	0.793

Adjusted R^2 = 0.93, n = 372.
** $P < 0.05$.
* $P < 0.10$.
LCC = land capability class.

approximately 93 percent of the variation in the dependent variable. Among the land-use share variables, only the forest share is significantly related to the percentage of the county in core forest. As expected, the sign of the coefficient is positive. We find also, and as expected, a positive and significant relationship between core forest and shares of land in public uses. Many of the land quality variables are significantly different from zero and, as expected, positive. Higher shares of land in lower LCC classes increase the amount of core forest relative to the highest LCC class. The range in elevation and the share of wealthy households do not have significant effects on the core forest share. Among the transition probabilities, only the agriculture-to-forest transition probability has a significant effect. As expected, counties with a higher probability of agricultural land moving to forest have more core forests.

The estimation results for the like adjacencies model are presented in table 6. The adjusted R-squared statistic for this model is 23 percent. Four of the coefficients on the land-use share variables are significantly different from zero at the 10 percent level or lower. As expected, like adjacencies are increasing in the forest share and declining in the agricultural and urban shares. Unexpectedly, we found a positive and significant relationship with the pasture share. None of the coefficients on the public land or the land quality variables are significantly different from zero. However, the coefficient on the elevation range variable is significantly different from zero. The sign is positive, indicating that greater elevation range is associated with less fragmentation. We expected the opposite relationship.[6] The agriculture-to-forest and forest-to-urban transition probabilities had negative and significant effects on like adjacencies. Although the second relationship has the anticipated sign, the first is contrary to our expectations. Finally, the like adjacencies are increasing in the share of wealthy households. Again, the sign of this coefficient is opposite from what we expected.

Comparing the results for the models, we find that the coefficients on only two variables were significantly different from zero in both models. The share of land in forest is positively related to the core forest and like adjacency metrics. The agriculture-to-forest transition probability has a significant effect on both fragmentation measures, but the signs of the effects differ between the two models. It has a positive effect on core forest and a negative effect on like adjacencies.

Discussion

The results of this analysis are mixed. The core forest model has a good fit and the coefficients of many explanatory variables are significant and have the expected signs. In contrast, the variables in the like adjacency model have relatively low explanatory power and many of the coefficients have unexpected signs. These results highlight the challenges inherent in estimating aggregate models of forest fragmentation. Forest fragmentation is the outcome of a spatial process. We have attempted to model fragmentation by using aggregate data that necessarily mask underlying spatial relationships. Moreover, we have used relatively large observational units (counties) in order to consider a large geographical area (11 Western States). Given our study area, it was infeasible to construct explanatory variables that summarize spatial patterns, such as the land-quality metrics used in Alig et al. (2005). Rather,

Among the land-use share variables, only the forest share is significantly related to the percentage of the county in core forest. As expected, the sign of the coefficient is positive. We find also, and as expected, a positive and significant relationship between core forest and shares of land in public uses.

---

[6] The earlier studies by Butler et al. (2004) and Alig et al. (2005) did not include a variable for elevation range.

Table 6—Estimation results for the like adjacency model

Variable	Coefficient	Standard error	t-value	P-value
Intercept	113.06**	14.62	7.73	<0.001
Share of crops	-0.12*	0.07	1.84	0.066
Share of pasture	0.26*	0.15	1.67	0.096
Share of forest	0.04**	0.01	2.88	0.004
Share of urban	-0.18**	0.04	-4.15	<0.001
Share of Conservation Reserve Program	-0.28	0.28	-0.98	0.329
Share of range	0.004	0.01	0.37	0.71
Share of federal forest land	0.01	0.01	0.79	0.431
Share of nonfederal public forest land	0.05	0.04	1.33	0.185
Share of nonfederal land in LCC II	-0.16	0.16	-1.00	0.319
Share of nonfederal land in LCC III	-0.10	0.15	-0.66	0.507
Share of nonfederal land in LCC IV	-0.08	0.14	-0.55	0.582
Share of nonfederal land in LCC V	-0.02	0.15	-0.12	0.904
Share of nonfederal land in LCC VI	-0.15	0.14	-1.03	0.303
Share of nonfederal land in LCC VII	-0.09	0.14	-0.65	0.517
Share of nonfederal land in LCC VIII	-0.15	0.14	-1.06	0.291
Per-county range of elevation	0.002**	0.001	3.47	<0.001
Agriculture-to-forest transition probability	-16.50**	8.33	-1.98	0.048
Only public forest	-5.24	4.25	-1.23	0.218
Forest-to-agriculture transition probability	-714.68	577.65	-1.24	0.217
Forest-to-urban transition probability	-115.41*	62.82	-1.84	0.067
Share of wealthy households	0.21*	0.11	1.81	0.072

Adjusted $R^2 = 0.23$, $n = 372$.
* $P < 0.05$.
** $P < 0.10$.
LCC = land capability class.

we relied on aspatial measures of land use, ownership, land quality, and land-use transition probabilities.

The share of land in forest was found to have a positive and significant effect on the percentage of the landscape in core forest and the percentage of like adjacencies for forest. This finding is related to a concept in landscape ecology referred to as the percolation threshold (Grimmett 1989). In the context of forest land, the idea is that once forests occupy a critical share of a landscape (approximately 60 percent), the number of spatially isolated patches drops at a fast rate with the addition of new forests. Thus, we find that an increase in the forest share, all else equal, increases both the fragmentation indices.[7]

---

[7] The foregoing discussion suggests a nonlinear relationship between the fragmentation indices and the forest share. We estimated models that included the square of the forest share and found negative and significant coefficients on this variable. Otherwise, the results were similar.

Other variables also have significant effects on forest fragmentation. In the core forest model, these include the public ownership and land-quality variables and the agriculture-to-forest transition probability. In the like adjacencies model, the crop and urban shares and the forest-to-urban transition probability had negative and significant effects. Three variables (pasture share, elevation range, and agriculture-to-forest transition probability) had significant effects but coefficients with unexpected signs. There are plausible explanations for the positive effect of elevation range and the negative effect of the agriculture-to-forest transition probability. Counties with large elevation ranges may have high mountains. In this case, agricultural and urban uses may be infeasible owing to steep slopes or prohibited by statute and, thus, forests may be less fragmented. Transitions from agriculture to forest may create isolated forest parcels, which could lower the like adjacencies variables. The pasture share may proxy for county characteristics in a way that is difficult to identify. This illustrates an inherent problem with aggregate data models and with our use of relatively large observational units. With smaller units, the predictive power of aggregate forest fragmentation models increases (Butler et al. 2004).

Our use of data on Western counties gives rise to other challenges with developing aggregate models of forest fragmentation. According to the data on like adjacencies, forest fragmentation is not a pervasive feature of Western forests. For approximately 69 percent of the counties, the like adjacencies measure exceeds 99 percent. For 88 percent, the measure exceeds 95 percent. This indicates that a large majority of the forest parcels in our study area are surrounded by other forest parcels (i.e., are core forest). The lack of variation in the like adjacencies variable makes it difficult to find significant explanatory variables. The fact that most forest parcels are core forest implies that the percentage of a county in core forest will closely correspond to the total share of the county in forest. Thus, our model is similar to a forest land shares model (e.g., Ahn et al. 2000) and may not provide many insights into the determinants of forest fragmentation.

Chapter 4: Spatially Explicit Fragmentation Analysis

We summarize the spatial pattern of the simulated landscapes by using the same forest fragmentation indices used in the aggregate model. This allows us to compare predictions of forest fragmentation measures produced with the two approaches.

In this chapter, we predict changes in forest fragmentation by using spatially explicit simulations. This approach differs markedly from the analysis in chapter 3, which uses an aggregate model of forest fragmentation. The analysis in this chapter uses the econometrically estimated transition probabilities, discussed in chapter 2, in a landscape simulation employing geographic information system (GIS) data on land use and parcel characteristics. We summarize the spatial pattern of the simulated landscapes by using the same forest fragmentation indices used in the aggregate model. This allows us to compare predictions of forest fragmentation measures produced with the two approaches. This comparison is the subject of chapter 4.

Methods

We conducted the analysis of forest fragmentation in Polk County, Oregon, by using the methods developed in Lewis (2005). Polk County is located in the Willamette Valley west of Salem, Oregon. We analyzed a 304,692-acre section of the county.[1] According to the Oregon Rural Lands Database (ORLD) (Oregon Department of Land Conservation and Development, n.d.), 41.5 percent of the land in our study area was in forest in 1998, 55.2 percent was in agricultural uses, 2.5 percent was in urban uses, and 0.8 percent was in other uses (table 7). The land-use transition probabilities for Polk County were extracted from the land-use projection model discussed in chapter 2.[2] The probabilities account for endogenous price feedbacks and, thus, are the same ones used (for Polk County) to produce the projections in chapter 2. There is very little land in the rangeland and Conservation Reserve Program (CRP) categories in Polk County. As well, the GIS data we used in the simulations do not identify pasture as a separate category. Therefore, we combined these uses with cropland and created a new category for all agricultural land. The transition probabilities indicate the probability that land moves from one

---

[1] The total land area of Polk County is 474,296 acres. We analyzed a portion of the county because our GIS data are available in U.S. Geological Survey quads, and we considered only those quads contained entirely in the county.

[2] We used the model parameters estimated in the national econometric analysis and the independent variables for Polk County to compute the transition probabilities. Separate probabilities are obtained for starting and ending use and land quality class, corresponding to the LQ variable used in the econometric analysis (see page 4). Given the national scope of the econometric analysis, we cannot account for all of the factors that influence land-use decisions in Polk County, including localized land-use regulations. However, our purpose in this section is to compare projections using different methods. In this regard, it is most important that we model a consistent set of land-use determinants.

Table 7—Simulation results for Polk County, Oregon

Categories	Forest share	Core forest share	Like adjacencies
Initial values (1998)			
Forest	41.5	35.3	94.3
Agriculture	55.2	48.3	95.7
Urban	2.5	2.0	93.6
Mean simulated values (2022)			
Forest	42.6	32.6	91.1
Agriculture	39.4	28.9	90.3
Urban	17.3	9.8	82.7

Note: 0.8 percent of the land is in uses other than forest, agriculture, and urban in 1998 and 2022.

use to another over the period 1997 to 2002. These 5-year probabilities are reported in the top half of table 8. The probability that high-quality (class 1) agricultural land remains in agriculture is 91.7 percent, compared to 94.8 percent for class 2 agricultural land. The probability that agricultural land transitions to forest is 4.3 percent for class 1 land and 2.1 percent for class 2 land. We would expect class 1 agricultural land to have a lower probability of converting to forest than class 2 land. We find that class 1 land is more likely to transition to forest because of the relatively high probability that class 1 pasture, which is included in the agriculture category, transitions to forest. The probabilities that class 1 and 2 agricultural land transitions to urban use are 4.1 percent and 3.1 percent, respectively. The transition probabilities for class 3 and 4 agricultural land are unimportant for our analysis because little agricultural land is found in these categories. The results for land initially in forest reveal very small probabilities for forest-to-agriculture conversions. Forest land has the highest probabilities of remaining in forest (between 94.6 percent and 97.7 percent) and converting to urban use (between 1.8 percent and 5.2 percent). Finally, we do not observe land transitioning from urban to other uses. Therefore, the urban-to-urban transition probability is assumed to equal one.

The simulations are conducted over the 25-year period, 1997 to 2022. Thus, we are ultimately interested in the likelihood that a parcel beginning the simulation in one use moves into the other uses by the end of the simulation. Assuming that the 5-year transition probabilities apply in each of the intervening periods, we can compute the transition probabilities for the 25-year period by iterative multiplication of the transition probability matrices for each land quality class. The results are presented in the bottom half of table 8. The results show, for example, that class 1 land in agriculture in 1997 has only a 64.8 percent probability of still being in

Table 8—Land-use transition probabilities for Polk County, Oregon

	Ending use		
Land quality	Agriculture	Forest	Urban
	Five-year transition probability (1997-2002)		
Initial use is agriculture			
1	.917	.043	.041
2	.948	.021	.031
3	.863	.099	.038
4	.863	.099	.038
Initial use is forest			
1	.002	.946	.052
2	.002	.954	.043
3	.003	.975	.021
4	.005	.977	.018
	Twenty-five-year transition probabilities (1997-2022)		
Initial use is agriculture			
1	.648	.160	.191
2	.766	.088	.146
3	.482	.356	.162
4	.483	.358	.159
Initial use is forest			
1	.009	.757	.234
2	.010	.792	.199
3	.011	.885	.103
4	.018	.896	.086

agriculture by 2022 and 16.0 percent and 19.1 percent probabilities of being in forest and urban, respectively. The probability that forest land remains forested after 25 years ranges from 75.7 percent to 89.6 percent.

Landscape simulations were conducted by using GIS data for Polk County. We obtained spatial data layers from the ORLD that categorize the landscape by agriculture, forest, and urban use and land quality classes 1, 2, 3, and 4.[3] By overlaying these data, we identified unique parcels that match the transition probabilities. For example, a given parcel may be identified as class 2 land that is initially in agriculture. In this case, we assume the parcel has a 76.6 percent probability of remaining in agriculture over the 25-year horizon and 8.8 percent and 14.6 percent

[3] A third data layer on land ownership is used to eliminate public lands, as the transition probabilities primarily represent land-use changes on private land.

probabilities of converting to forest and urban use, respectively (table 8). The landscape simulations are conducted by using a random number generator. The number generator randomly selects a value from the uniform distribution defined on the unit interval. For the parcel discussed above, if the selected value is below 0.766, the parcel remains in agriculture, if it falls between 0.766 and 0.854 the parcel is converted to forest, and if it is between 0.854 and 1.0 the parcel converts to urban. For every parcel on the landscape, we match the land quality and initial land use of the parcel to the relevant transition probabilities and repeat the simulation procedure. The result is a simulated landscape that is consistent with the underlying transition probabilities assumed to govern land-use change.[4]

Given the probabilistic nature of the transition rules, there are a large number of landscapes that are consistent with the rules. Generating all of these landscapes[5] would be time consuming and produce results that are difficult to interpret. We handled this challenge in two steps. First, we summarized the spatial pattern of forest land by using fragmentation metrics computed with the Fragstat software. The use of fragmentation metrics reduces the number of unique outcomes because many different landscapes will produce the same value of a given fragmentation index. The fragmentation metrics include the percentage of the landscape by use, the percentage of the landscape in core forest (defined as a forest patch more than 100 feet from the nearest nonforest edge), and the percentage of like adjacencies for forest. The latter metrics are computed in the same way as those used in the aggregate fragmentation analysis. Second, we ran 500 simulations in order to characterize the range of possible outcomes.[6] In particular, we computed empirical frequency distributions defined over values of the fragmentation indices.

Results

Simulation results are presented in table 7 and figures 2 through 4. We project an increase in forest area from 41.5 percent of the land base to 42.6 percent, on average, by 2022. Figure 2 shows that the distribution of the forest share is roughly symmetrical, with values ranging from approximately 40 percent to 44.5 percent. The share of land in urban use is projected to increase substantially, from 2.5 percent to 17.3 percent, while the agricultural land share declines from 55.2 percent

---

[4] The probabilities are from an econometric analysis employing data from a random sample of plots. This prevents us from accounting for factors such as spatial correlation among land-use decisions and parcelization.

[5] If there are X parcels and Y uses, then there are Y^X possible landscape configurations.

[6] Extensive diagnostics, discussed in Lewis (2005), were done to determine the appropriate number of simulations.

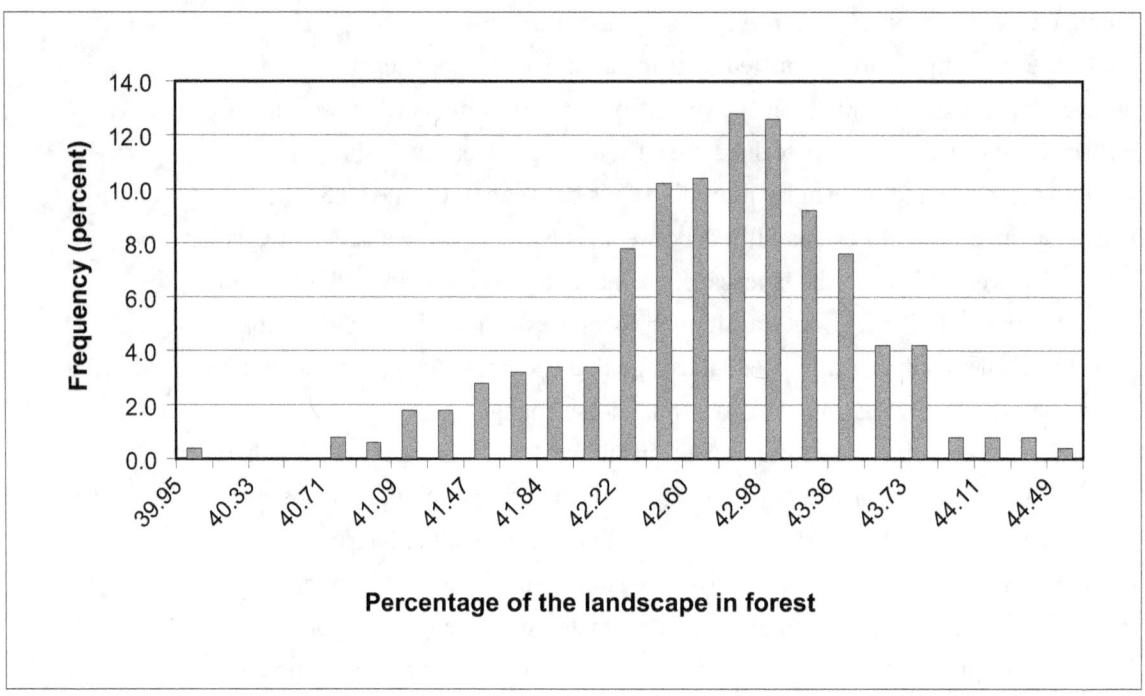

Figure 2—The percentage of the landscape in forest from simulation results for Polk County, Oregon, 2022.

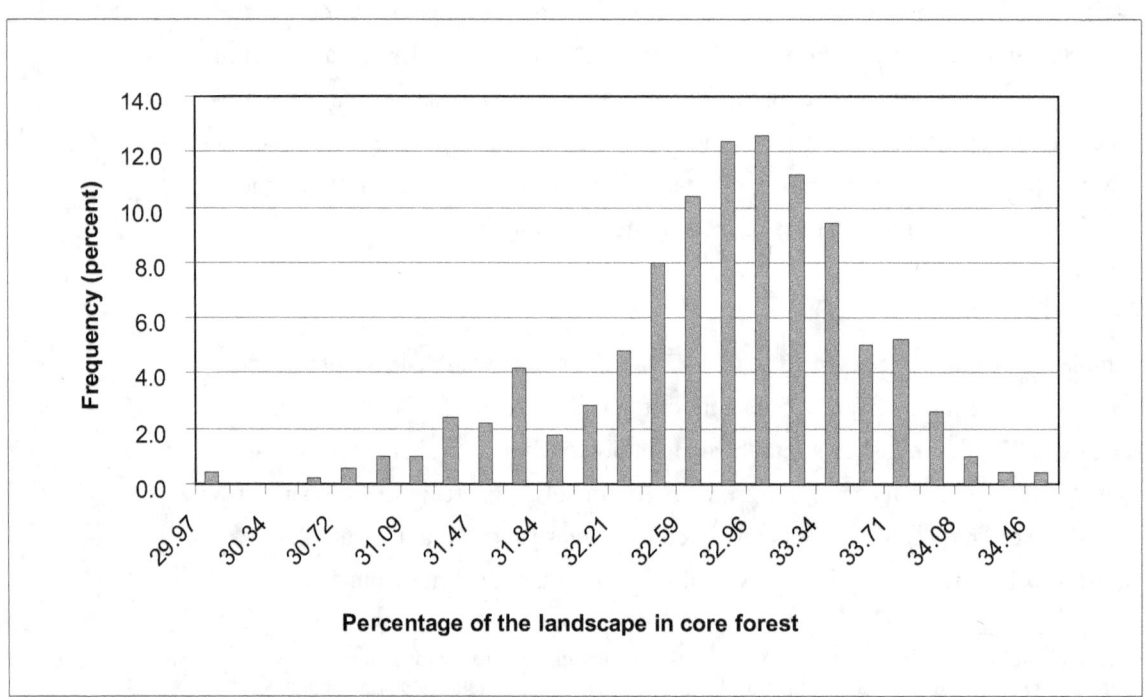

Figure 3—The percentage of the landscape in the core forest from simulation results for Polk County, Oregon, 2022.

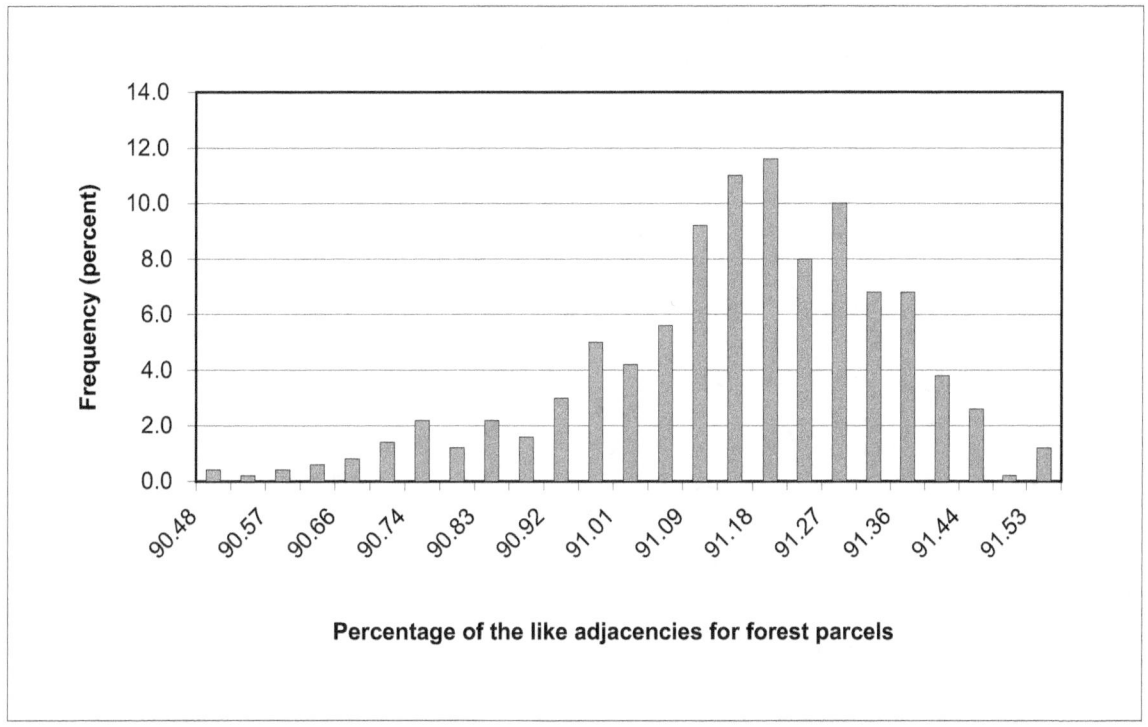

Figure 4—The percentage of the like adjacencies for forest from simulation results for Polk County, Oregon, 2002.

to 39.4 percent. Despite the increase in forest area, we project the percentage of the landscape in core forest to decline from 35.3 percent to 32.6 percent, on average, with values ranging from approximately 30.0 percent to 34.5 percent (fig. 3). Likewise, the percentage of like adjacencies for forest is projected to decline from 94.3 percent to 91.1 percent, on average, with values ranging from about 90.5 percent to 91.5 percent (fig. 4).

These results show that increases in forest area need not reduce the degree of forest fragmentation.[7] The forest share increases by 1.1 percentage points, but we find that the expected share of the landscape in core forest declines by 2.7 percentage points, suggesting that some of the new forest parcels are relatively small or isolated from existing forest patches. Another possibility is that fragmentation results from the conversion of existing forest land to urban use, which increases by almost 15 percentage points over the projection period. Moreover, the statistics in table 7 reveal that urban land in Polk County becomes more dispersed over time. Using the same definition of a core parcel as used for forest land, we computed

These results show that increases in forest area need not reduce the degree of forest fragmentation.

---

[7] Our simulation results depend to some degree on initial landscape conditions. See Lewis and Plantinga (in press) for a treatment of this issue.

the share of core urban land. In 1998, 80 percent of the urban land was in core (2 percent divided by 2.5 percent), but by 2022, this share has dropped to 57 percent. Similarly, the percentage of like adjacencies for urban land was 93.6 percent in 1998, declining to 82.7 percent by 2022. The increase in urban area, coupled with more dispersed urban land, can account for the increase in forest fragmentation. A similar explanation can be offered for the change in the percentage of like adjacencies for forest, which is projected to decline by 3.2 percentage points.

Chapter 5: Linkage of Land-Use Projections and Fragmentation Models

In this chapter, we link the land-use projections and the aggregate fragmentation analysis. The shares of land in crops, pasture, forest, urban, Conservation Reserve Program, and range are included as explanatory variables in the fragmentation models. Thus, we can estimate how the fragmentation metrics will change as the shares of land in different uses change. We use projections of county land-use shares to estimate the share of land in core forest and the percentage of like adjacencies for forest in 2030. As well, we project these indices for Polk County, Oregon, to the year 2022 to compare the results from the aggregate and spatially explicit analyses.

County Projections of Fragmentation Metrics

Using observed and projected values of the county land-use shares, we used the estimated parameters in tables 5 and 6 to compute fragmentation metrics for 1997 and 2030. We present the results in two ways. First, we computed percentage changes (1997 to 2030) in average state-level values. The state averages are formed by averaging the predicted values over counties within each state. The core forest measure is projected to increase in 8 of the 11 states (table 9). Declines are found in

The core forest measure is projected to increase in 8 of the 11 states. Declines are found in the three Pacific States (California, Oregon, and Washington) and relatively large increases are found for Arizona and New Mexico.

Table 9—Projected changes in the core forest and like adjacency metrics for Western States, 1997 to 2003

State	Core forest share	Like adjacencies for forest
	Percentage change, 1997-2030	
Arizona	12.3	0.2
California	-4.4	-0.8
Colorado	3.2	0.2
Idaho	6.4	1.1
Montana	5.9	0.0
Nevada	7.2	0.0
New Mexico	22.8	0.9
Oregon	-2.5	-0.8
Utah	2.9	-0.2
Washington	-4.0	-0.2
Wyoming	11.6	-0.1

Note: To arrive at these figures, we first averaged the county-level measures to obtain a state average for 1997 and 2030. Then, we computed the percentage change in the state average.

the three Pacific States (California, Oregon, and Washington) and relatively large increases are found for Arizona and New Mexico. To some degree, the changes in the core forest metric correspond to the projected changes in the share of land in forest. The three Pacific States have negative or small positive projected changes in the forest share. Relatively large percentage increases in forest are projected for Arizona and New Mexico. For the like adjacency measure, small changes in the state averages (between -0.8 percent and 1.1 percent) are projected. Increases are projected in four states, with the largest percentage gains in Idaho and New Mexico (table 9). As indicated in table 6, increases in crop and urban shares reduce the like adjacency measure and increases in forest and pasture increase it. Differences among the state-level changes in like adjacencies are due to the specific patterns of land-use change.

The second way to present the results is with maps revealing changes for each county (figs. 5 and 6). For the core forest metric, declines in the metric for counties in western Oregon and Washington are apparent. The increases in Arizona and New Mexico are not as readily seen because of the way in which the categories are defined. For the like adjacency metric, increases are apparent for counties in California, Nevada, Oregon, and Washington, and declines can be seen in Arizona, Montana, Wyoming, and New Mexico.

Comparison of Fragmentation Projections by Using Spatially Explicit and Aggregate Methods

The spatially explicit and aggregate approaches to projecting fragmentation metrics rely on the same transition probabilities derived from econometric analysis of National Resources Inventory data (chapter 2). Moreover, the aggregate model of forest fragmentation is estimated with observations on western counties, including Polk County, Oregon. Therefore, we can compare the projection results for Polk County generated with the two approaches. But, first, we must make some adjustments to the fragmentation metrics. Public forest lands are included in the county-level measures used in chapter 2, but excluded from the measures used in chapter 4. If we assume that all public forests are core forest and have 100 percent like adjacencies, then the initial percentage of all private lands in Polk County in core forest is 42.0 percent and the initial percentage of like adjacencies for these forests is 96.6 percent.[8] These figures differ from those computed for the 304,692-acre section of

---

[8] The core forest share of all land in Polk County is 53.7 percent. We subtract the public forest land share (11.7 percent) to obtain 42 percent. The like adjacency measure for all forest is 97.3 percent. Public forests represent 19.6 percent of all forests and so the like adjacency measure for private lands is given by (97.3 − 19.6)/80.4 = 96.6 percent.

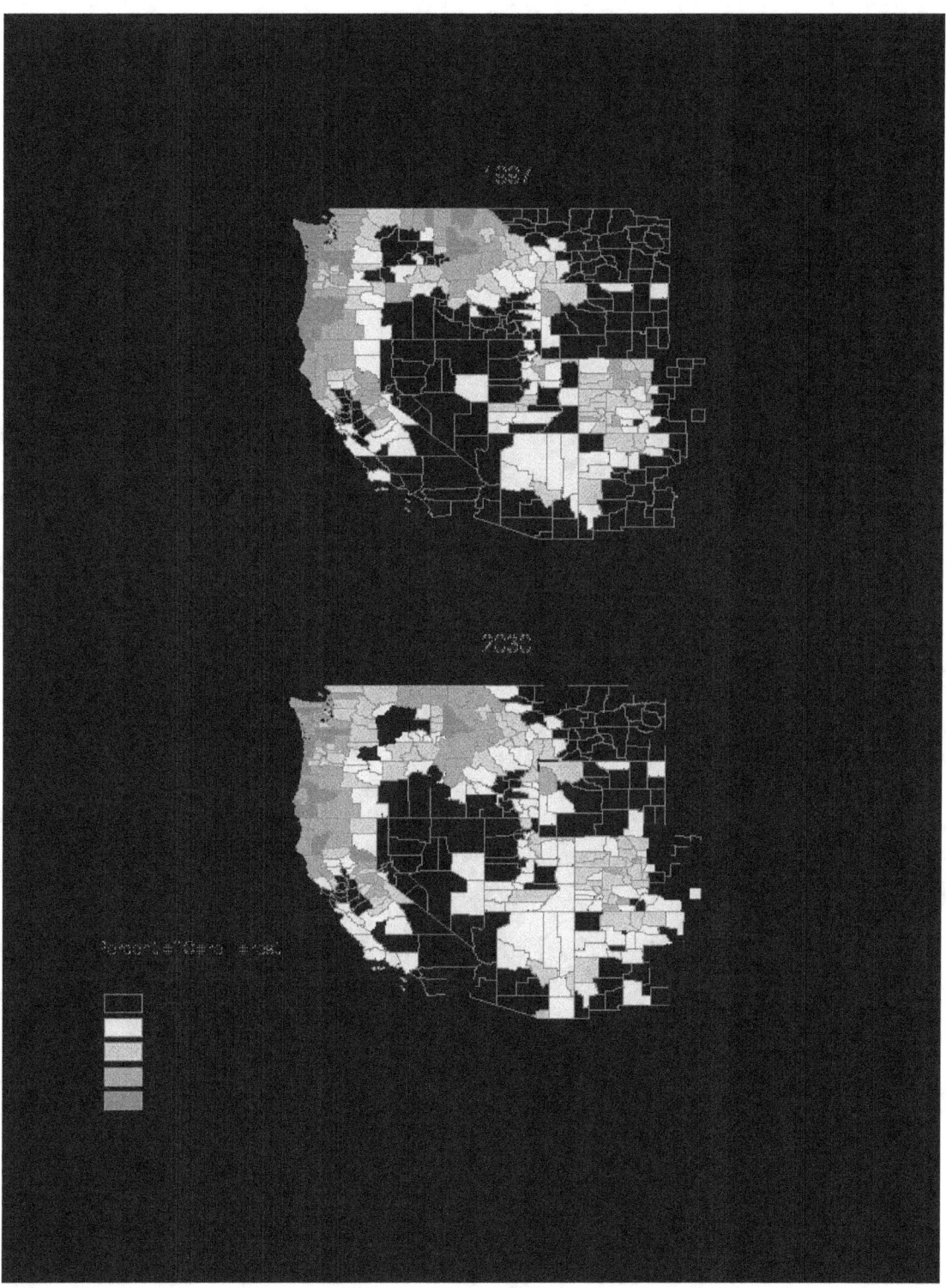

Figure 5—The share of the landscape in core forest in Western U.S. counties, 1997 and 2030.

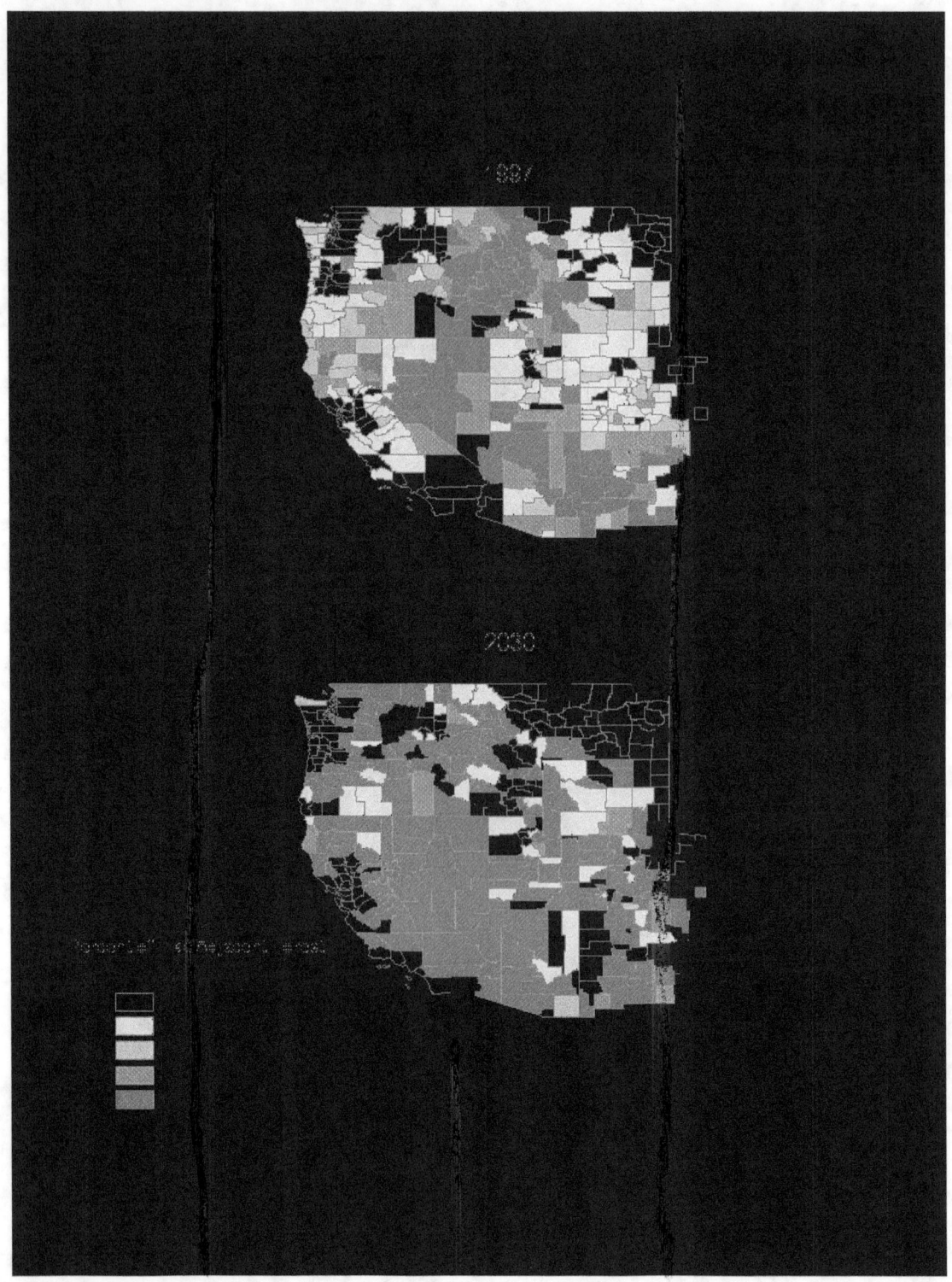

Figure 6—The percentage of like adjacencies for forest in Western U.S. counties, 1997 and 2030.

Polk County analyzed above. As noted in chapter 4, the initial core forest and like adjacency measures are 35.3 percent and 94.3 percent, respectively.[9]

Because the initial values differ, we compare percentage changes in the fragmentation metrics. Based on the aggregate model, we project that the core forest share of private lands in Polk County will decline by 4.0 percent by 2022. The corresponding figure from the spatially explicit analysis ranges from 2.4 to 15.1 percent, with a mean value of 7.6 percent. Thus, the prediction from the aggregate model falls within the range of outcomes generated with the spatially explicit analysis (fig. 3). However, the predicted 4.0 percent decline is an "outlier" in the sense that it is found in the tail of the distribution. Ninety-five percent of the distribution is found between 4.5 percent and 11.4 percent. Using the aggregate model, we project only a 0.1 percent decline in the like adjacency measure for all private forests in Polk County by 2022. The spatially explicit analysis yields declines in the range of 3.0 to 4.0 percent and, thus, we find that the two methods produce considerably different results. Nevertheless, given the differences in the methods used, it is noteworthy that the projected changes in the fragmentation metrics have the same sign and are the same order of magnitude in percentage terms.

---

[9] There may simply be differences in the fragmentation of forests within and outside the section of the county considered.

Chapter 6: Summary and Conclusions

We use an econometric model of private land-use decisions to project land use to 2030 for each county in the continental United States. We assume that net financial returns to urban, pasture, and range remain constant through time, but allow crop and forest returns to adjust endogenously to the projected changes in land use. On a national scale, forest area is projected to increase between 1997 and 2030, representing a change overall between 0.1 and 0.2 percent per year. Urban area is projected to increase by 68 million acres over this period, with annual increases ranging from 1.6 to 2.7 percent. Cropland, pasture, rangeland, and Conservation Reserve Program land is projected to decline by 2030.

> **We found that the share of the county in core forest increases with the shares of land in private, federal, and other public forest. This finding may reflect the concept from landscape ecology of a percolation threshold. Once the area occupied by forest is sufficiently high, patches become connected and fragmentation is reduced.**

The national projections were disaggregated by Resources Planning Act (RPA) regions. Increases in forest area are projected for the Corn Belt, Mountain, Pacific Northwest East, Northern Plains, and South Plains. The largest increases occur in the Mountain and South Plains regions (10.3 and 8.0 million acres, respectively). Declines are found for the other regions, with the largest occurring in the Southeast and Northeast (3.6 and 3.0 million acres, respectively). The finding of forest area increases in predominately agricultural regions was unexpected. However, the National Resources Inventory data for the period 1992 to 1997, which were used in the estimation of the econometric model, reveal significant shifts of rangeland to forest in the Mountain region and pasture to forest shifts in the Corn Belt and South Central regions. Additional research is warranted along with augmentation of land-use data pertaining to transitions among major land uses. First, regional econometric models can be estimated that might better represent relationships specific to the region. Second, the land-use projection model can be modified to account for endogenous price responses to changes in pasture and rangeland. This would likely reduce transitions into forest by raising the opportunity costs of converting pasture and rangeland.

We conducted an analysis of forest fragmentation in the Western United States. One of the primary goals was to determine if county-level forest fragmentation metrics can be modeled in terms of aggregate variables constructed from readily available data, in contrast to using spatial data that are more costly to obtain. For the core forest model, many of the proposed explanatory variables were significantly different from zero and have coefficient signs consistent with expectations. We found that the share of the county in core forest increases with the shares of land in private, federal, and other public forest. This finding may reflect the concept from landscape ecology of a percolation threshold. Once the area occupied by forest is sufficiently high, patches become connected and fragmentation is reduced. We also found that the core forest percentage increased with lower quality land and a higher agriculture-to-forest transition probability.

The results for the like adjacency model are weaker. As expected, the like adjacency metric was positively related to the forest share and negatively related to the agricultural and urban shares and the forest-to-urban transition probability. However, we found positive effects from the pasture share, greater elevation range, and the share of wealthy households and a negative effect from the agriculture-to-forest transition probability. The last four results are contrary to expectations. One of the challenges with modeling like adjacencies is that this variable exhibits relatively little variation in the Western United States. For approximately 69 percent of the counties, the like adjacencies measure exceeded 99 percent, indicating very little forest fragmentation (at least at the scale considered) in the majority of counties. This is an important empirical finding in its own right and motivates the search for alternative representations of forest fragmentation that may confirm this finding. Also, it may be of interest to compute the like adjacencies measure for other U.S. regions (e.g., the Midwest and Northeast) where it is expected to be lower.

Another challenge—common to both fragmentation models—is how to appropriately model an inherently spatial phenomenon by using aggregate variables. A promising approach is to include explanatory variables that summarize spatial pattern within the unit of observation (counties, in our case). Alig et al. (2005) found that indices summarizing the spatial configuration of land quality were a significant determinant of forest fragmentation. One might also use this approach to represent the spatial configuration of urban land, which is likely to be a factor in determining forest fragmentation but is unlikely to be correlated with traditional measures of land quality. Another strategy is to reduce the geographical scale of the observations (e.g., from counties to census tracts). However, this increases the cost of the analysis.

We conducted a spatially detailed analysis of forest fragmentation in Polk County, Oregon. This approach has much greater data requirements, and considerable computing resources are needed to conduct land-use simulations. One of the interesting findings is that forests in Polk County are projected to become more fragmented even though forest area increases. The amount of core forest, for example, will not necessarily increase if new forest parcels are isolated from existing or other new forest parcels. Moreover, there may be an overall decline in core forest if enough existing core forest parcels are converted to nonforest uses such as urban. This finding for Polk County is consistent with the aggregate fragmentation analysis. Although the county-level fragmentation metrics depended positively on shares of land in forest, other variables, such as urban shares, were found to have negative effects.

We linked the land-use projections and the analyses of forest fragmentation. County land-use shares were included in the aggregate forest fragmentation models, allowing us to determine how projected changes in land use would affect the fragmentation metrics. We found increases in the average county shares of core forest in 8 of the 11 Western States, with the largest percentage changes in New Mexico, Arizona, and Wyoming. The average like adjacency measure increased in six of the states. Declines were found in all of the Pacific Coast States. One of the valuable features of this approach is that we can examine changes in the spatial distribution of the fragmentation metrics by using geographic information system-based maps.

We compared the results of the aggregate and spatially detailed fragmentation analyses. In each case, we projected the fragmentation indices to 2022. Both approaches rely on the same land-use transition probabilities and measures of forest fragmentation, and evaluate conditions in Polk County, Oregon. We found considerable differences in the results produced with the two methods, especially in the case of the like adjacency metric. This finding may indicate that the aggregate data method, which does not account explicitly for spatial processes, is invalid. It should be noted, however, that we were unable to design a perfect test. Owing to the nature of the available data, the spatially detailed analysis considered only a portion of Polk County, whereas the aggregate model included the entire county. Additional research could evaluate aggregate fragmentation models estimated at a finer scale, such as census tracts (e.g., Alig et al. 2005, Butler et al. 2004). This would provide a closer correspondence between the geographical areas evaluated under the two approaches.

Forest fragmentation is an important cause of biodiversity loss in terrestrial ecosystems. We have developed a framework for modeling forest fragmentation at large scales and projecting changes in fragmentation under different economic and policy scenarios. Our analysis directly supports the Sustainable Wood Production Initiative and the RPA assessments, and expands efforts to define and develop protocols for sustainable forest management. Moreover, our approach offers promise for analyzing emerging policies designed to reduce forest fragmentation. Our econometric model quantifies the relationship between net returns to alternative land uses and land-use transitions. As such, the model can be used to simulate the effects of market-based policies, such as subsidies, encouraging conversion of land to forest or retention of land in forest. The effects on landscape-level indicators of forest fragmentation can then be measured by using the procedure discussed in

Forest fragmentation is an important cause of biodiversity loss in terrestrial ecosystems. We have developed a framework for modeling forest fragmentation at large scales and projecting changes in fragmentation under different economic and policy scenarios.

chapter 4. Lewis and Plantinga (in press) developed an application of this approach to South Carolina. Using the models developed here, a national-scale policy analysis could be conducted.

Metric Equivalents

1 foot = 0.3048 meters
1 yard = 0.9144 meters
1 acre = 0.4047 hectares

Acknowledgments

The authors thank Brett Butler, Ruben Lubowski, Susan Stewart, and Eric White for helpful comments and suggestions.

References

Adams, D.M.; Haynes, R.W. 1996. The 1993 timber assessment market model: structure, projections, and policy simulations. Gen. Tech. Rep. PNW-GTR-368. Portland, OR: U.S. Department of Agriculture, Forest Service, Pacific Northwest Research Station. 58 p.

Ahn, S.; Plantinga, A.J.; Alig, R.J. 2000. Predicting future forest land area: a comparison of econometric approaches. Forest Science. 46(3): 363–376.

Alig, R.; Butler, B. 2004. Forest cover changes in the United States: 1952 to 1997, with projections to 2050. Gen. Tech. Rep. PNW-GTR-613. Portland, OR: U.S. Department of Agriculture, Forest Service, Pacific Northwest Research Station. 106 p.

Alig, R.; Kline, J.; Lichtenstein, M. 2004. Urbanization on the U.S. landscape: looking ahead in the 21st century. Landscape and Urban Planning. 69(2-3): 219–234.

Alig, R.; Lewis, D.J.; Swenson, J.J. 2005. Is forest fragmentation driven by the spatial configuration of land quality? The case of western Oregon. Forest Ecology and Management. 217: 266–274.

Alig, R.; Plantinga, A.J. 2004. Future forestland area: impacts from population growth and other factors that affect land values. Journal of Forestry. 102(8): 19–24.

Alig, R.; Plantinga, A.; Ahn, S.; Kline, J. 2003. Land use changes involving forestry in the United States: 1952 to 1997, with projections to 2050. Gen. Tech. Rep. PNW-GTR-587. Portland, OR: U.S. Department of Agriculture, Forest Service, Pacific Northwest Research Station. 92 p.

Armsworth, P.R.; Kendall, B.E.; Davis, F.W. 2004. An introduction to biodiversity concepts for environmental economists. Resource and Energy Economics. 26: 115–136.

Butler, B.J.; Leatherberry, E.C. 2004. America's family forest owners. Journal of Forestry. 102(7): 4–9

Butler, B.J.; Swenson, J.J.; Alig, R. 2004. Forest fragmentation in the Pacific Northwest: quantification and correlations. Forest Ecology and Management. 189: 363–373.

Deal, R.L.; White, S.M. 2005. Understanding key issues of sustainable wood production in the Pacific Northwest. Gen. Tech. Rep. PNW-GTR-626. Portland, OR: U.S. Department of Agriculture, Forest Service, Pacific Northwest Research Station. 67 p.

Goodwin, B.K.; Brester, G.W. 1995. Structural change in factor demand relationships in the U.S. food and kindred product industry. American Journal of Agricultural Economics. 77(1): 69–79.

Grimmett, G. 1989. Percolation. New York: Springer-Verlag. 296 p.

Lewis, D.J. 2005. Managing the spatial configuration of land: the economics of land use and habitat fragmentation. Corvallis, OR: Oregon State University. 138 p. Ph.D. thesis.

Lewis, D.J.; Plantinga, A.J. [In press]. Policies to reduce habitat fragmentation: combining econometric models with GIS-based landscape simulations. Land Economics.

Lubowski, R.N. 2002. Determinants of land-use transitions in the United States: econometric analysis of changes among the major land-use categories. Cambridge, MA: Harvard University. 172 p. [plus appendices]. Ph.D. thesis.

Lubowski, R.N.; Plantinga, A.J.; Stavins, R.N. 2006. Land-use change and carbon sinks: econometric estimation of the carbon sequestration supply function. Journal of Environmental Economics and Management. 51(2): 135–152.

Moulton, R.J.; Richards, K.R. 1990. Costs of sequestering carbon through tree planting and forest management in the United States. Gen. Tech. Rep. WO-58. Washington, DC: U.S. Department of Agriculture, Forest Service. 44 p.

Oregon Department of Land Conservation and Development. [N.d.] Oregon rural lands database. http://geography.uoregon.edu/infographics/rldatabase/. (July 13, 2006).

Riitters, K.H.; Wickham, J.D.; O'Neill, R.V.; Jones, K.B.; Smith, E.R.; Coulston, J.W.; Wade, T.G.; Smith, J.H. 2002. Fragmentation of continental United States forests. Ecosystems. 5: 815-822.

Train, K. 2003. Discrete choice methods with simulation. Cambridge, England: Cambridge University Press. 334 p.

U.S. Department of Agriculture, Forest Service. 2001. 2000 RPA assessment of forest and range lands. FS-687. Washington, DC. 78 p.

White, H. 1980. A heteroskedasticity-consistent covariance matrix estimator and a direct test for heteroskedasticity. Econometrica. 48: 817-838.

Appendix—Variable Measurement and Data Sources

Land Use

The land-use data used to estimate the econometric model are from the USDA National Resources Inventory (NRI). "Croplands" include row and close-grown crops, fallow, pasture and haylands in rotation with crops, permanent haylands, vineyards, orchards, and nurseries. "Pasture" includes land managed for introduced forage for livestock grazing. "Range" includes land under native or introduced forage suitable for grazing which, unlike pasture, receives only limited management. "Forests" are areas at least 1 acre in size and 100 feet in width that are at least 10 percent stocked with trees with the potential to reach 13 feet at maturity. This translates to a canopy cover of at least 25 percent. "Urban lands" include areas in residential, industrial, commercial, or institutional uses. Parcels below 10 acres, such as small parks and transport facilities, are also classed as urban if they are completely surrounded by urban lands. This definition excludes roads and other lands used for transportation in nonmetropolitan areas, as these are separately identified by the NRI.

Net Returns for Rural Land Uses

Estimated annual cropland net returns per acre consist of two components: a weighted average of the net returns for 21 major crops and total federal farm program payments, excluding payments from the Conservation and Wetlands Reserve Programs. We used state-level marketing-year-average prices and county-level yields from the National Agricultural Statistics Service (NASS) for 21 major crops. Cash costs at the state and regional levels, respectively, are from the Census of Agriculture and Economic Research Service (ERS). County acreages from NASS and the Census of Agriculture provided weights. County-level estimates of total federal direct farm program payments per acre are from the Census of Agriculture and include receipts from deficiency payments, support price payments, indemnity programs, disaster payments, and soil and water conservation projects.

Annual net returns per acre for pasture were estimated by using yields from the National Cooperative Soil Survey (NCSS). We multiplied yields by the state price for "other hay" for NASS and deducted costs for hay and other field crops from the Census of Agriculture.

Annual net returns per acre for rangeland were estimated with forage yields from NCSS multiplied by state-level per head grazing rates from the ERS database on cash rents.

Annual net returns per acre from forestry were constructed by annualizing at a 5 percent interest rate the estimated net present value of a weighted average of sawtimber revenues from different forest types. State-level stumpage prices were gathered from state and federal agencies and private data services. Regional timber yields for different forest types were obtained from Richard Birdsey of the USDA Forest Service. Regional replanting and management costs were derived from Moulton and Richards (1990). An infinite stream of timber revenues for each forest type was estimated by using the optimal rotation age from the Faustmann formula. County acreage and sawtimber output data from the Forest Inventory and Analysis and Timber Product Output surveys of the U.S. Forest Service provided weights for averaging across individual forest types and species, respectively.

Urban Net Returns

Annual urban net returns were estimated as the median value of a recently developed one-acre parcel used for a single-family home, less the value of structures, annualized at a 5 percent interest rate. Median county-level prices for single-family homes were constructed from the Census of Population and Housing Public Use Microdata Samples and the Office of Federal Housing Enterprise Oversight House Price Index. Regional data on lot sizes and values of land relative to structures were obtained from the Characteristics of New Housing Reports (C-25 series) and the Survey of Construction microdata from the Census Bureau.